The Woman's Cry For Khilafah

Dr. Nazreen Nawaz

مكتبة اسلامية MaktabaIslamia

MaktabaIslamia Publications

www.maktabaislamia.com
info@maktabaislamia.com
www.facebook.com/everythingislamic
www.twitter.com/maktabaislamia
www.telegram.me/maktabaislamia

2017 CE – 1438 H

Translation of the Qur'ān

It should be perfectly clear that the Qur'ān is only authentic in its original language, Arabic. Since perfect translation of the Qur'ān is impossible, we have used the translation of the meaning of the Qur'ān throughout the book, as the result is only a crude meaning of the Arabic text.

Qur'ānic verses appear in speech marks proceeded by a reference to the Surah and verse number. Sayings (*Hadith*) of Prophet Muhammad ﷺ appear in inverted commas along with reference to the Hadith Book and its Reporter.

ﷺ - صلى الله عليه وسلم (Peace be upon him)

ﷻ - سبحانه وتعالى (Glory to Him, the Exalted)

Contents

The Situation for Muslim Women in the Absence of the Khilafah

In 2005, the Gallop Organization conducted a survey entitled, *"What Women Want: Listening to the Voices of Muslim Women"*. Over 8000 face-to-face interviews were conducted with women in eight predominantly Muslim countries including Jordan, Turkey, Pakistan, Saudi Arabia, Egypt, and Morocco. When asked what they resented most about their own societies, a majority of Muslim women polled stated that a lack of unity amongst the Muslim nations, violent extremism and political and economic corruption were their main concerns. An overwhelming majority of the women cited, "attachment to moral and spiritual values" as the best aspect of their own societies and saw the adoption of Islam rather than Western values as the path to the Muslim world's political and economic progress. The Khilafah or Caliphate State that implements the Islamic Shariah upon a society and is based purely upon laws extracted from the Islamic texts is the embodiment of this vision.

Such findings may raise the question as to why so many women would wish to live under a state that has been described by a number of Western politicians and intellectuals as highly oppressive to women. Tony Blair in his now infamous 16th of July 2005 speech to the Labour Party national conference following the 7/7 bombings described the caliphate state as one where, *"Girls (are) put out of school. Women denied even rudimentary rights. People living in abject poverty and oppression. All of it justified by reference to religious faith..."*. The journalist Peter Hitchens wrote in an article in the Mail on Sunday (17th September 2006), *"These are the facts....The more Islamic a state is, the more its women are shrouded and confined, the more its minorities are despised and the more freedom of thought and speech are crushed."* Houzan Mahmoud, the UK head of the Organisation of Women's freedom in Iraq described an Iraqi constitution that would have Islam as its source and basis, *"A recipe for future gender enslavement, second-class citizenship and ignorance...Women in Iraq face being dragged back into the dark ages...".*

For a century and more, the Khilafah state has been presented by many Western intellects and indeed some Muslim thinkers, writers and politicians as a state where women are subjugated to violence, discriminated against, rendered to second-class citizens, enslaved to men, denied education or basic economic and political rights such as the right of employment or the vote and live in a state of fear.

However, this description is more befitting of what has become of the lives of millions of Muslim women across the Muslim world in the absence of the Khilafah over the last 80 plus years.

Women Affected by Occupation:

Muslim women have become the terrorised victims of colonial wars in Iraq and Afghanistan. In the current blood-bath of the Iraq war, women and children constitute half of the 655,000 innocent civilians killed at the hands of Coalition forces. They have faced mindless slaughter at the hands of gun-ho US soldiers as in Falluja, Haditha, and Ishaqi. The victims of the Haditha massacre in May 2006 where 24 were killed, included women and five children between the ages of 14 and 2. The Ishaqi massacre in March 2006, where 11 civilians were shot dead in their house, execution-style included four women and five children amongst whom was a six month year old baby and seventy-five year old grandmother. Women have been shot at coalition checkpoints, such as thirty-five year old Nabiha Nisaif Jassim, who was killed last year by US soldiers. She was a heavily pregnant woman who was in labour at the time and being rushed to a maternity hospital.

This state of violence has been coupled with the sexual humiliation suffered by Iraqi women at the hands of coalition forces. How can we forget the Abu Ghraib experience where Muslim women were sexually tortured in the same manner as the men, forced to undress in front of male guards, photographed, and some raped. In March 2007, five US soldiers in the town of Mahmudiya were involved in the rape and murder of 14 year old Abeer Qassim Hamza. They then proceeded to murder her mother, father and 5 year old sister execution style and to set the body of the 14 year old on fire to cover their crime. It seems that Western governments and coalition forces have stepped into Saddam's shoes as the new terrorisers of Iraqi women.

The lives of women in occupied Iraq has become one of daily misery and strife. Many do not have access to basic needs such as clean water, healthcare, and medicines; one in four are dependent on food aid; old women widowed and childless as a result of the war, beg on street corners; young girls are sold into prostitution; women and girls are prisoners of their own home - too scared to go to school, university or work from fear of being abused, abducted or raped. According to the UN, rapes have quadrupled between 2003 and 2006. During Saddam's time, women were scared of stepping out of line. Now women fear stepping out of their houses.

In Afghanistan, Muslim women and children continue to be the victims of sustained military action by NATO, US and British forces. According to the UN, 380 civilians have been killed in the first four months of 2007 alone. Many have been women and children. Almost six years post-invasion and under a secular regime, 90% of women remain illiterate; one woman dies every 30 minutes from pregnancy-related diseases; only 30% of girls have access to education; one in five children die from preventable diseases; and the average life expectancy for women in Afghanistan is 44 years (figures from IRIN).

The charity "Womankind Worldwide" states that 60-80% of the people in Afghanistan live on less than 1 dollar a day and commented in their 2006 report that, *"It cannot be said that the status of Afghan women has changed significantly in the last 5 years"*. Matt Waldman, the Oxfam head of policy for Afghanistan in a recent Guardian article (May 26th, 2007) described the desperate poverty in which Afghanis in the Daikundi province live. He described children chewing on mud they scratch from the walls to stave off their hunger. With all the rhetoric of the "liberation of women" to part justify the wars on Afghanistan and Iraq, it seems that the only things that have been "liberated" are the oil and gas routes through Central Asia and the Middle East.

In the Muslim world, women have also undergone and continue to experience indescribable suffering from decades of occupation in Palestine, Chechnya and Kashmir with no hope of help nor liberation by the cowardly rulers and regimes currently governing the Muslim world. Arbitrary arrest, illegal detention, disappearance, torture, sexual violence, rape, death, and destruction are everyday occurrences in these lands. In Palestine, many pregnant women are detained at checkpoints or prevented from reaching hospitals and clinics by the Israeli military occupation force. Consequently, women are forced to give birth at checkpoints; women and new born babies are dying at checkpoints; the unborn are dying in their mothers wombs. In Chechnya and Kashmir, soldiers breaking into houses, kidnapping, gang-raping and killing women and girls is an everyday reality according to independent human rights organizations.

Across the Muslim world, thousands of women endure a daily struggle for economic and physical survival under the strangulating economic policies of global capitalism. Privatization of public resources, crippling interest-based loans, and manipulation of local economies to maximise profits of Western Transnational Corporation and governments at the expense of developing nations have subjected many women in Muslim countries to dire poverty.

The consequence is lack of funding for the provision of basic needs, education, healthcare, or employment opportunities. This is despite the fact that the cost of providing basic healthcare and nutrition for every person throughout the world each year is less than the annual expenditure in Europe and the US on pet food. Thousands of women have been enslaved into sweat shops in Indonesia, Bangladesh, and Pakistan working long hours in hazardous environments for $1/day to maintain the huge profit margins of multi-billion capitalist companies. It appears that within the capitalist ideology, there is economic benefit in perpetuating injustice.

Women Facing the Injustice of Un-Islamic Regimes and Traditions in the Muslim World

Coupled with this reality is the political and economic corruption and total incompetancy of the regimes of the Muslim lands. The Muslim world is governed by dictatorial rulers whose primary aspirations lie in squandering the wealth of the land on lavish lifestyles and securing their thrones of power rather than investing in the economic growth and development of their countries and citizens. Consequently, it is not surprising that the Muslim countries have some of the worst illiteracy rates for women in the world: Bangladesh - 80%; Pakistan - 64%; Egypt - almost 1 in 2 women are illiterate (figures from UN).

Alongside this economic deprivation is the general oppression facing Muslim women in many of the societies of the Muslim lands due to tribal and pre-Islamic traditions, laws and culture: discrimination in access to education, employment, and justice; rape victims languishing in jails; political rights non-existent in some countries; forced marriages; stove burnings due to marital disputes; honour killings - hundreds in Pakistan, Jordan, and Turkey alone; thousands of women in Bangladesh hospitalized each year from nitric acid thrown onto their faces for refusing a marriage suitor or disputes regarding dowry; and the list goes on.

These oppressive customs have been given fertile ground to grow and strengthen through governing systems within various Muslim countries that embody these non-Islamic tribal and pre-Islamic laws. Saudi Arabia, Iran, Nigeria, Pakistan and other states within the Muslim world are monarchies, theocracies, and secular dictatorships whose structure of ruling have no association with the Islamic texts and therefore with the Khilafah system.

Jordan's constitution for example states that the killing of individuals in the name of honour is not a crime. In Pakistan, women who have been raped are often treated by the system as the guilty party rather than the victims of a hideous crime. Alongside this oppression is the overt discrimination within a number of secular Muslim states such as Turkey and Tunisia, where Muslim women wearing the hijab and fulfilling an Islamic obligation have been denied the right to enter universities and public institutions, impeding their educational aspirations and societal contributions.

The rise in tribal and cultural views within certain communities in the Muslim world regarding women is also due to an era of decline in Islamic thoughts and values within Muslim societies resulting from the absence of the Khilafah system. The rights afforded to women within the Islamic civilization of the past and prescribed within the Islamic texts are well documented by both Muslim and non-Muslim writers and historians: the right to education, employment, the vote and the right to voice her opinions regarding the issues of her society, choice in marriage and the right of divorce, inheritance, the rights of citizenship on par with the men of society and importantly, the right to respect, security and protection of her honour and life. However, unlike Western societies where suffragette and other women's movements often had to battle the system to ensure their rights were secured, the rights afforded to women in the societies of Islamic history were dependent upon the Khilafah system. When the application of this system weakened or worse still disappeared then these rights could no longer be guaranteed.

Can adopting Secular Liberalism or Capitalism Liberate the Muslim Woman?

It is often suggested that the Muslim woman would be liberated by the adoption of secular liberal values in the Muslim societies or the modelling of the governing systems in the Muslim world upon the Western secular model. However, the daily lives of many women living within Western secular liberal nations is far from enviable or liberated. In the US, a woman is sexually assaulted every 2 ½ minutes (US Department of Justice), in the UK 50,000 women were raped last year and 1 in 20 women have been raped in England and Wales (British Crime Surveys 2002 and 2006). In the UK, 54% of women have experienced sexual harassment one time or another during their careers (Work Foundation). In the US, a woman is battered every 20 seconds and domestic violence is the second highest cause of homicide (US Department of Justice). In the UK, the police receive a call every minute from a victim of domestic violence and 1 in 4 women have been beaten by their husbands or partners.

Despite more women in the workforce, more women in political office, even legislation to protect the rights of women, the question needs to be asked how much attitudes and views in Western secular nations towards women have really changed since the emergence of the suffragette movements a century ago. The extent of these problems suggests that the cause cannot simply be placed at the feet of a handful of perverse men in the society but questions need to be asked about some of the values held within secular capitalist societies that nurture an environment that gives rise to such views and degrading behaviour towards women.

The Devaluing of Women within the Capitalist System:

Within the capitalist system, the drive for profit reigns supreme and has been weighted over humanity. This has led to even the bodies of women being given a price tag. The pursuit of the dollar or the pound has given freedom of expression the permit to exploit the bodies of women through pornography or the advertising and entertainment industries. What affect is expected on the security and respect for women in the workplace and in the general society when this view of the woman as a sexual object to fulfill the desires or fantasies of men is promoted within the society?

It perhaps explains why being a doctor, lawyer, politician, or even a policewoman is not a barrier to sexual harassment. The honour of women has become an insignificant casualty of the capitalist money-making machine. The black writer Audre Lorde once wrote,*"Whatever we do takes place in a social context and has an affect upon other human beings. To degrade someone, even with that person's expressed consent, is to endorse the degradation of persons. It is to affirm that the abuse of persons is acceptable."*

However, a question should also be raised regarding the massive demand for pornographic material within liberal societies. Why in Britain are over 20 million pornographic magazines sold each year? Why in the US does pornography generate a revenue of over $13 billion - exceeding the combined revenues of the ABC, CBS, and NBC channels? David Wilson, Professor of Criminology at the University of Central England in Birmingham raised an important point in a Guardian article regarding government proposals to ban the possession of violent pornography on the internet. He wrote, *"We need to tackle the demand for abusive and violent images on the internet and not just their supply."*

This demand is based upon particular liberal values propagated within secular societies such as personal freedom - the idea that an individual can live and act according to his whims and desires. It therefore has the potential of facilitating the right of a man to view and treat a woman according to his desires. Coupled with the sexualization of society through provocative images of women on billboards, adverts, magazines, and in the entertainment industry on the premise of freedom of expression, it has produced a lethal cocktail for society and disastrous affects upon the lives of ordinary women.

Within such a reality it may not be surprising that boys as young as 13 are on the sex offenders register for raping girls of 9 or 10. It may not be surprising that in the US, 3 women die each day from domestic violence. It may not be surprising that there are large numbers of men fathering children but rejecting any responsibilities towards them, resulting in spiralling rates of single mothers. It may not be surprising that the value that women are given within society has reached such a low that violent pornography - gaining pleasure from viewing the abuse and torture of women has become an entertainment past time for many men, fuelling murders such as that of Jane Longhurst - raped and strangulated by a man who had spent hours viewing such images.

The Pursuit of the Body-Perfect and its Consequences on Society:

Alongside such attitudes towards women within liberal secular societies are other problems affecting women. The obsession with beauty, fashion and the pursuit of the body perfect has had a crippling affect upon the self-esteem of many women in the West. The constant pressure to measure up to unrealistic man-made expectations of beauty, figure size and shape has created paranoia within many women about their appearance. It has even led to many women not having the confidence with their bodies to enter public life. A survey by "Dove" the beauty brand last year found that 1 in 4 girls between the ages of 15 and 17 avoid normal activities such as school, work, visiting the doctor or job interviews due to insecurity regarding their appearance. Furthermore, these irrational ideals have contributed to an epidemic of eating disorders. In the UK, over 1 million women suffer from an eating disorder. In the US, 1 in 100 girls between 10 and 20 suffer from Anorexia Nervosa (US National Institute of Mental Health).

This obsession with beauty within western societies has led to many judging the success of women, deciding promotions, and even employment appointments upon looks rather than their skills. The well known Western feminist Germaine Greer, wrote in her book, "The Whole Woman", *"Every woman knows that, regardless of all her other achievements, she is a failure if she is not beautiful."* A society cannot promote beauty as one of the most important aspects of the woman and then not expect discrimination in work or public life based upon appearance.

The Devaluing of Family Life Within Capitalist Societies

Within capitalist societies, gender discrimination in the workplace continues to be a real problem. A survey by the "Recruitment and Employment Confederation" in November 2005 found that 3 in 4 companies would rather break the law than employ a pregnant woman or one of child-bearing age. In 2006, the Equal Opportunities Commission predicted that 1 million pregnant women are likely to experience discrimination at work over the next 5 years, based upon current figures of pregnancy-related discrimination - everything from pay cuts, demotion, being fired, or even pressure to terminate the pregnancy. Under a capitalist system, the constant focus on short-term profitability over all else, including family values has nurtured an environment where home-life is devalued and where many employers fail to appreciate the importance of family responsibilities. Consequently, a woman with young children or who becomes pregnant is often viewed as a burden to their company rather than an asset to the society. It is an ideology that has placed profit over people, finance over families.

Within the society, work for many women is not often a choice but has become an essential requirement due to financial or societal pressures to measure up to the successful career woman. Consequently, many women have been forced to choose between raising their families or earning a living - to adopt the identity of the "superwoman" - struggling to juggle a successful career with marital and family responsibilities - constantly stressed and frustrated she feels that she cannot give adequate attention to either nor provide adequate time for herself. This has strained many marriages and contributed to the breakdown of family life within the society. In the UK over 50% of single mothers live below the poverty line. Under a capitalist system that has failed to provide sufficient financial support for women to choose to stay at home and care for their children, these same mothers have been financially pressured into work, leaving others to raise their children. This has contributed to the rise of dysfunctional families that many politicians have described as a major cause of widespread anti-social behaviour amongst the youth.

Western Governments Seek to Export Secularism as the Model for Women's Liberation:

As evident from the above discussion, the idea that women in the Muslim world could be liberated by adopting liberal, secular, or capitalist values or systems is to simply exchange one set of problems for another. Today, Western governments are seeking to export the secular ideology as the model for the liberation of women in the Muslim world. However, this call for "women's rights for Muslim women" by a number of Western politicians is well recognised as nothing but a smokescreen to conceal colonial intentions in the Muslim world. It has become familiar rhetoric used to simply justify the invasion of countries and interfere in the politics of Muslim lands to prevent the return of the Khilafah state. For example, the call for the liberation of the Muslim woman by Western politicians is often accompanied by derogatory remarks regarding the Islamic political system and its treatment of women.

Talk of "women's rights" carries little weight by governments who supported the Northern Alliance into power in Afghanistan - an organization notorious for its gang-rapes of women; or governments who have no qualms in cosying up to Saudi princes - governing over a country where women are not even permitted to drive; or governments who ally themselves with dictators such as Islam Karimov of Uzbekistan - who has imprisoned grandmothers for simply asking for justice for their sons or challenging the corruption of their state.

Islam and the Khilafah State Create a status of Honour for Women:

In Islam the woman is viewed as an honour to be protected at all times. The Prophet (saw) said on one occasion,

"The world and all things in the world are precious but the most precious thing in the world is a virtuous woman."

Islam obliges every man to view the woman in this way whether it is his mother, sister, daughter or any woman within the society - Muslim or non-Muslim. This is surely how every woman, Muslim and non-Muslim deserves to be viewed. In his last sermon, the Prophet (saw) said,

"Fear Allah regarding the woman. Verily you have married them with the trust of Allah and made their bodies lawful with the words of Allah."

The man is therefore obliged to treat the woman upon this premise of honour and responsibility and not according to his desires.

In addition, there are numerous Islamic evidences that aim to build a high status for the woman in society as a mother, wife or daughter in contrast to the belief often propagated that Islam belittles the woman or views her inferior to the man. The value that Islam gives to the woman in these various roles should also nurture an environment of respect in the manner that she is viewed and treated within family life and the society.

Regarding the status of the daughter, the Prophet (saw) said,

"Whosoever has a daughter and he does not bury her alive, does not insult her, and does not favour his son over her, God will enter him into paradise."

In another hadith, he(saw) said,

"Whoever has three daughters and shelters them, provides what they need and shows compassion towards them, will certainly deserve Paradise." A man among the people asked, "And if they are two, O Messenger of Allah?" And he said, "Yes, even if they are two".

Regarding the status of the wife, the Prophet (saw) said,

"The believer who has the most perfect faith is the one whose behaviour is the best and the best of you are the ones who are best to their women" (al-Tirmidhi).

In his last sermon, the Prophet (saw) said,

"O People, it is true that you have certain rights, with regards to your women but they also have rights over you. Remember that you have taken them as your wives only under Allah's trust and with His permission. If they abide by your right then to them belongs the right to be fed and clothed in kindness. Do be kind to them for they are your partners and committed helpers."

Regarding the status of the mother, the Prophet (saw) said,

"Paradise lies beneath the feet of the mother". A man at the time of the Prophet (saw) came to him and said "I have carried my mother single handed around the Kaba 7 times, does this repay the kindness she showed me as a child?" The Prophet replied "It does not even repay one contraction of the womb".

It was narrated that on one occasion a woman called Salamah said to the Prophet (saw),

"O Messenger of Allah, you brought tidings to men but not to women." He said, "Did your women friends put you up to asking me this question?" She said, "Yes, they did." He (saw) said, "Does it not please any of you that if she is pregnant by her husband and he is satisfied with her that she receives the reward of one who fasts and prays for the sake of Allah? And when the labour pains come none in heaven or earth knows what is concealed in her womb to soothe her. And when she delivers, not a mouthful of milk flows from her and not an instance of child's suck, but that she receives, for every mouthful and every suck, the reward of one good deed. And if she is kept awake by the child at night, she receives the reward of one who frees seventy slaves for the sake of Allah."

(narrated by Anas(ra); Tabarani).

How the Khilafah System Creates a Status of Honour for the Woman:

The Islamic political system does not approach the organisation of society on the basis of securing individual freedom but on the basis of securing particular rights for every citizen - male or female, Muslim or non-Muslim without distinction. These include protection of people's beliefs, property, lives and honour - what are termed as the maqasids or aims of the shariah. Islam therefore does not believe in the freedom of a man to view or display a woman's body in any way that he desires, to have relations with a woman and father her children with no responsibility to her nor her child, to commit adultery and betray his wife and family, or to express his anger in marriage by harming his wife - whether through beating, burning, or throwing acid onto her body.

Slanderous accusations against the chastity, honour and therefore reputation of the woman is a serious criminal offence, punishable under the law. The Qur'an states, *"And those who launch a charge against chaste women, and produce not four witnesses (to support their allegations), flog them with eighty stripes; And reject their evidence ever after: for such men are wicked transgressors."* [24:4]. It was narrated that on one occasion during the life of the Prophet (saw), a man called Hilal accused his wife of adultery. The Prophet (saw) said to him,

"Bring your proof or fear the lash upon your back".

Hilal replied to him that he had witnessed the act himself. The Prophet (saw) responded again,

"Bring your proof or fear the lash upon your back",

 for the burden of proof in trying cases of adultery must be no less than four witnesses seeing the actual act of intercourse. Therefore, honour killings by which women are killed upon mere conjecture of guilt by individuals who have adopted the position of judge and executioner are clearly prohibited within Islam and under the Khilafah state. Infact, those individuals who mar the reputation of women through slanderous accusations may be the ones who find themselves at the firm end of the law.

It is this view of the woman as an honour that is built, propagated and protected within the Khilafah state. Therefore, it is not simply legislation that prohibits a woman from being beaten, abused, exploited, harassed or raped but rather the value that society gives to the chastity, honour and reputation of the woman. No action would be permitted to compromise this. For example, the exploitation of a woman's beauty or the sexualization of society for economic or other gain through pornography or provocative adverts, magazines, TV shows or otherwise is absolutely prohibited. All this would cheapen the view of the woman within society and lay a foundation that would undermine the chastity of individuals. There is zero tolerance to any form of sexual harassment whether verbal, physical, or even by innuendo. Sexual abuse and rape are of course extremely serious crimes with weighty punishments for those found guilty, to deter others from engaging in such hideous acts.

Historical Examples of How the Khilafah Protected the Honour of Women:

Within the history of the Khilafah state, there are numerous examples of how seriously the Khalifahs viewed the honour of women in contrast to the cowardly rulers of the Muslim world today. Today, as Muslim women in Iraq, Kashmir, Chechnya and beyond are abused and raped; as they hide their faces in shame; as their wombs carry the proof of their dishonourment, the Muslim rulers stand muted and paralysed by their western masters. Their silence has been deafening. As Muslim women stripped of their dignity cry out for the Muslim armies to liberate their land from the claws of their oppressors, the Muslim rulers chain their armies to their barracks and lovingly embrace, harbour troops, protect bases, and supply the oil that feeds their occupiers' war machine.

It is a far cry from the Khalifahs of the past who did not tolerate the honour of one Muslim woman being defiled - leaders like Khalifah Mutassim Billah who within hours of receiving news that a Roman soldier had dishonoured a Muslim woman, saw it as his duty to respond as if it were an attack on the whole state - a diplomatic incident of the highest order warranting the firmest possible response. In the end he dispatched a force of 40,000 troops against nothing less than the strongest fort of the Roman Empire.

In the 8th century, when some Muslim women were taken as prisoner by the Raja of Delhi, Muhammad ibn Qasim was dispatched by the Khilafah with six thousand cavalry and six thousand armed cavalry drivers. He faced an army several times this size and defeated them. Can there be any doubt that the salvation and protection of Muslim women lies in the return of the Islamic Khilafah State?

Such examples of the Khilafah should not be surprising for the Prophet (saw) said in one hadith (narrated by Abdullah ibn Umar(ra),

"The ruler is the shade of Allah on earth; it is with him that the oppressed servants of Allah take shelter."

The Rights, Responsibilities and Role of Women within the Khilafah State

Within the Khilafah system whose constitution, canons, principles, and values are based purely upon the Islamic texts, women would play an active role to build a state that is not only morally elevated but also economically prosperous and scientifically advanced.

Education

Within Islam, the seeking of knowledge has been made compulsory on both women and men.   The Prophet (saw) said,

"The seeking of knowledge is an obligation upon the believing man and the believing woman".

Upon this basis, it is not only permitted for girls to have an education but rather it is an obligation upon the State to provide free education to boys and girls alike at primary and secondary level. This would include subjects such as mathematics, the experimental sciences such as biology or chemistry, languages as well as the Islamic disciplines. The Khilafah would strive to eradicate illiteracy amongst both men and women within the state. In addition, the state would encourage women to engage in higher studies to become for example doctors, scientists, architects, or scholars of Islam. We have the example of Sheikha Shuhda, who was a prominent scholar in the 11th century who lectured publicly in the largest mosque in Baghdad - the capital of the Khilafah at the time.

The Economic Sphere:

Within the economic sphere in Islam the woman is permitted to work. The Prophet (saw) has said,

"O women! You have been allowed by Allah(swt) to go out for your needs."

There are many examples of women engaging in economic transactions at the time of the Prophet (saw). His own wife Saudah for example was a businesswoman who would tan the skins of animals and sell them for large profits. A woman named Qilah would ask the Prophet (saw) various questions on how to run her business according to Islam. Therefore, within the Khilafah state, the woman is permitted to trade, invest her wealth, own property, work a business, lease property, be an employer or employee or undertake various other societal transactions. She could be an engineer, a nuclear physicist, or even a pilot. The woman can take an administrative post within the state or be appointed as a judge. The woman Ash-Shifa was appointed in the important post of Judge of the market place by Umar bin Al-Khattab, the second Khalifah of Islam. The woman would also play an active role within the media to ensure that the correct understanding of Islam is imparted to both the citizens of the state and to foreign nations. However, because the woman should always be viewed as an honour, the exploitation of the femininity or beauty of the woman within any profession is prohibited.

In addition, within Islam the woman is to be financially supported by the male members of her family, her community, and by the state which has the obligation of ensuring the provision of food, clothing, shelter, health care, and education to all its citizens - male and female without distinction. Therefore, although the woman is permitted to work, there should be no societal or financial pressures upon her to do so if she chooses not to for the woman cannot compromise her vital role of being a wife and mother, creating a tranquil family life, caring for her children and family and nurturing the thinking and development of the future generations. She does not have to embrace the long suffering identity of a superwoman, struggling to balance a successful career with a successful home life for her value within the society is based upon her obedience to her Creator and not upon the level of tax she contributes to the economy.

Politics:

In the political arena of life, Islam has obliged the woman to play an active role. The Prophet (saw) said on one occasion, addressing both the man and woman,

"You must command the good and forbid the evil and hold fast the hand of the tyrant ruler and limit him to the truth..."

Within the Khilafah, the woman would therefore play an important role within the politics of the state, accounting the ruler and removing the corruption from the society. She could be appointed as an official of the state in a non-ruling position. She would be encouraged to be a member of the various political parties present under the state or to be within the Majlis Al-Ummah - the consultative body that advises the ruler. In addition, unlike states such as Saudi Arabia, she would be involved in the electoral process to select a ruler, following in the footsteps of those women present in the delegation that gave the *ba'yah* (pledge) to Muhammad (saw), accepting him to be the leader of the first Islamic State.

Women within the Khilafah state cannot however hold a position of ruling.

This is established from Islamic evidences. Those who have failed to study the Islamic texts deeply have claimed that this is because Islam believes that the woman is not physically able to perform this action and have therefore labelled Islam as being discriminatory towards women and viewing them as inferior to the man. Islam has given no such reason but has simply prohibited this action for the woman. One should also understand that ruling in Islam is not a position of prestige but a position of responsibility. Status in Islam is not measured by the one who holds a position of responsibility but by how resolutely an individual fulfils any duty obliged upon him. A ruler by default does not hold superiority over a mother - both have responsibilities to fulfil to ensure the society prospers.

Perhaps, one should ask the question as to why women within secular states feel it necessary to enter positions of ruling. Is it perhaps due to the fact that within secular democracies she continues to have to fight for her rights since these are not automatically guaranteed by the system? In contrast, within Islam, the rights of the woman are enshrined within the Islamic texts and are not subjective to the view of the ruler. The woman therefore simply needs access to the accounting bodies of the state which the Khilafah provides to ensure that her rights are fulfilled by the ruler.

Ensuring a Safe Environment for the Woman in Public Life

Islam has defined a public role for the woman under the Caliphate but in contrast with secular states, it has also defined rules to enable her to fulfil this within a secure environment where she is viewed as an honour. This is achieved through the implementation of the Islamic social system within the society that regulates the relationship between men and women within the society. The Islamic dress code, the fact that beautification of the woman in public life is not permitted, the prohibition of socialising between the sexes, the prohibition of fornication or adultery are examples of rules that seek to ensure that when men and women interact in society, anything that may trigger the sexual desires does not compromise the cooperation of the sexes or the honour and chastity of individuals. The Islamic system seeks to take sexual relations and that which leads to it out of the equation in public life and direct it to marriage. Consequently, the beauty of the woman is also taken out of public life and directed to marriage. It aims to achieve an environment where the woman can have an active public life, be educated, work, trade and travel in a secure manner without being harassed or harmed as well as be judged based upon her abilities rather than her looks.

This would be the view and role of women within the Khilafah system. Is it not appropriate that the thinking individual therefore looks beyond the outdated allegations that have been made against Islamic governance: that it is oppressive, that it mistreats the woman, that it is barbaric. It is necessary to put to rest these outdated clichés and bring this discussion regarding the Khilafah and women into the 21st century. The hijab has often been labelled as a veil of oppression that needs to be discarded, however there has been a veil of lies surrounding the issue of Islam, the Khilafah and women for a number of centuries and it is this that needs to be discarded.

Germaine Greer, the embodiment of western feminism, wrote in her book "The Whole Woman", *"For years after The Female Eunuch was written I travelled the earth to see if I could glimpse a surviving whole woman. She would be a woman who did not exist to embody male sexual fantasies or rely upon a man to endow her with identity and social status, a woman who did not have to be beautiful, who could be clever, who would grow in authority as she aged."* Perhaps it would be wise to end her travels by examining the true status of women within Islam and the Khilafah system.

The Woman's Role in Working for the Khilafah

As Muslim women, we witness the suffering, abuse, rape and murder of our beloved mothers, sisters, daughters and Ummah every day. The Prophet (saw) said,

"The Muslims are like one body in their affection, compassion and sympathy towards one another, if one part suffered, the rest of the body reacts with sleeplessness and fever".

There is no doubt that each of us suffers from sleeplessness and aches from pain and grief knowing the distressed state of our brothers and sisters across the world. However, the Prophet (saw) also said that,

"The Muslim is the brother of the Muslim, he does not oppress him nor does he let him down. Whoever removes a wordly grief from a believer, Allah will remove from him one of the griefs of the Day of Judgement. Whoever shields a Muslim, Allah will shield him on the Day of Resurrection".

The believer is therefore not simply one who sheds tears as their Ummah suffers, their lands are torn apart and their *deen* attacked but rather someone who understands that they have a responsibility in removing the oppression from their brothers and sisters and to guard their *deen*. It is clear to understand that the widespread oppression of women in the Muslim world lies in the absence of the Khilafah state. It is also evident that the salvation of this Ummah lies in the establishment of this system. It alone can protect the dignity, lives and property of the Muslims and return the honour to our *deen*. It is "*Al-Ra'i*" - the guardian. The Prophet (saw) commented that,

"The Imam (leader/Khalifah) is the shield which protects the Muslims and behind which the Muslims fight".

Imam Nawawi explaining the meaning of this hadith said, "The imam is a shield means a protection because he prevents the enemies from hurting Muslims and prevents people from hurting each other".

The obligation for the Woman to Work for the Khilafah

Muslim women have a great responsibility alongside their brothers in Islam to work for the return of the Khilafah in the Muslim world. This obligation of carrying the *Da'wah* for the resumption of the Khilafah is no less a burden and priority for the believing woman than it is for the man. She has the same responsibility in striving and struggling with all her effort for its establishment. So in addition to fulfilling her important duties as a daughter, wife or mother, or her individual ibadat such as her prayer, fasting and Hajj, she must also never neglect this important obligation.

In Surah Anfal, Allah(swt) says,

"O you who believe! Answer Allah (by obeying Him) and (His) Messenger when he (peace and blessings be upon him) calls you to that which will give you life . . ."."
[TMQ Anfal: 24]

This verse is related to the duty of carrying the *Da'wah* of Islam to raise Allah(swt) word the highest. This is not simply *Da'wah* to call individuals to the Islamic belief but also *Da'wah* to call for the return of Allah's rule to the earth. It is clear that it is addressed to the believers as a whole and not restricted to men alone. In Surah Al-Maida, Allah(swt) says,

"And rule between them by that which Allah revealed to you and do not follow their vain desires away from the truth which came to you."   [TMQ Al-Maida: 48]

The verse calls upon Muslims to establish the rule of Allah(swt). Practically this can only be acheived by the establishment of the Khilafah. Again, the verse is general and addressed as an obligation to both the believing man and woman.

In one hadith reported by Abdullah bin Umar(ra), he said,

'I heard the Messenger of Allah(saw) say:

"Whosoever takes off his hand from allegiance to Allah(swt) will meet Him (swt) on the Day of Resurrection without having any proof for him, and whoso dies whilst there was no *Bay'ah* (allegiance) on his neck (to a Khalifah), he dies a death of *Jahiliyyah* (ignorance)'".

This hadith is again general in nature (i.e. "Whosoever...), addressed to all of the believers and not restricted to men. The hadith explains how the one who dies without the *Ba'yah*(pledge of allegience) on his or her neck dies the death of *Jahiliyyah*: the time before Islam. This indication of punishment after death contained within the hadith (i.e.dying a death of *jahiliyyah* which is associated with severe punishment) is the Qarina (indication) that it is an obligation for every muslim: scholar or learner, male or female regardless of where they live to have the *ba'yah* on his or her neck.

The *ba'yah* cannot be given to anyone except the Khalifah. Hence the woman and the man need to ensure that there is in existence a Khilafah system and Khalifah some where in the world to whom they can give the *ba'yah* to. If such a Khalifah is not present as is the case today then it becomes an obligation upon the neck of every Muslim to work to re-establish the Khilafah and appoint the Khalifah. This obligation is without difference for the man and woman.

The Method and Actions undertaken by the Woman to Establish the Khilafah

As with all obligations within Islam, the method of establishing the Khilafah state should be based upon evidences extracted from the Qur'an and the Sunnah. The method of the Prophet (saw) in establishing the first Islamic State in Madinah was based upon non-violent political action where he challenged the oppressive non-Islamic ideas, values, traditions and laws within the society and presented the Islamic thoughts, values, solutions and system as the alternative way to organise and govern a state. It is therefore this method that should be adopted for changing the non-Islamic societies and systems in the Muslim world to one based upon the ideology and rule of Islam.

Although we may live in Britain, as Muslim women there are many styles that we can utilise to aid the return of the Khilafah in the Muslim world. We can raise discussions of the need for the Khilafah state with our families, friends, teachers or colleagues - explaining how this alone will resume Islam as a way of life in the Muslim lands. We can raise similar discussions at gatherings in our houses, in the mosque, or in community centres. As mothers, meetings with other mothers can be used as opportunities to talk about the plight of mothers and sisters across the world and the need for the Khalifah to protect the honour of the Ummah and our *deen*.

Many of us are originally from the Muslim world and as such we may have large extended families or many friends who are still there, in countries such as Pakistan, Bangladesh, Indonesia, the Arab world, Turkey, or Central Asia.

Alternatively, we may come into contact and befriend Muslims who have come to the West temporarily for many reasons such as study, training, work, or on holiday, planning to return after a specified time. By discussing with such people, we could directly facilitate the return of the Khilafah. We may ourselves visit the Muslim lands and should use this great opportunity to carry the *Da'wah* to our family, friends, and contacts directly. We may have family, friends, or contacts abroad who are in the Muslim army, or who are politicians, journalists, writers, lecturers at university, judges, or community leaders. These are individuals that we have an added responsibility to discuss with for they may have influence over the people within the society and could play a vital role in facilitating the establishment of the state.

As Muslim women, we also need to be at the forefront of eradicating the lies about women and the Khilafah to the non-Muslim community. We need to dismantle the web of deception woven around Islam, explaining to our neighbours, friends, and colleagues the true status of women under the Shariah and to relay the fact that women globally deserve a better deal than their current status under capitalist secular states.

Finally, as a Muslim woman and as a representative of Hizb ut-Tahrir, I call you sisters to support and work with our organisation in this most honourable of actions to bring back the Khilafah State so that we may once again return the dignity that is deserving to this Ummah and to our *deen* and that will herald the birth of a new horizon of justice and light for this world.

Following the Footsteps of the Noble Female *Da'wah* Carriers of the Past

By engaging in this work to establish Allah(swt) rule on earth, the Muslim woman is treading the path of those many noble women and sahabiyat of the past who carried the *Da'wah* to Islam. They mirrored the men in their enthusiasm, courage and sacrifice in working to establish the authority of Islam in Makkah and beyond. They were women praised by our beloved Prophet (saw) and many were promised paradise.

Women such as Khadija bint Khawaylid(ra), the first wife of the Prophet (saw) supported the *Da'wah* of the Messenger(saw) until her dying breath and faced all the hardships that it involved with courage, even witnessing the suffering of her own children in the cause. The Prophet (saw) said of her,

"I have not yet found a better wife than her. She had faith in me when everyone, even members of my own family and tribe did not believe me, and accepted that I was truly a Prophet and a Messenger of Allah(saw). She converted to Islam, spent all her wealth and worldly goods to help me spread this faith, and this too at a time when the entire world seemed to have turned against me and persecuted me."

Khadija(ra) in her childhood had been brought up in luxury in her wealthy father's home but bore with patience the severe economic boycott suffered by the early Muslims at the hands of the Quraysh, even when at times there was nothing to eat but the leaves of trees. Infact it was through the high regard that she was held in Makkah that on occasions some of her non-Muslims contacts in Makkah brought food to the besieged Muslims. Such was her character that Allah(swt) himself sent salaams to her. In one hadith narrated by Abu Hurairah(ra), it was said that the Angel Gibril came to the Prophet (saw) and said,

"O Allah's Messenger! This is Khadija, coming to you with a dish having meat soup. When she reaches you, greet her on behalf of her Lord and on my behalf, and give her the glad tidings of having a palace made of Qasab in Paradise, wherein there will be neither any noise nor any toil."

(Bukhari)

Women such as Sumayyah bint Khabat(ra) experienced some of the most horrific torture at the hands of the Quraysh but never relinquished her belief in Islam nor the action of calling people to the worship of Allah(swt). When the mid-day heat was at its most intense, Abu Jahl would drag her, her son and husband out to an exposed area and place them on rocks scolding hot from the sun's rays. Other times they would pour burning sand over them, place heated shields on their bodies and throw heavy rocks at them. The Prophet (saw) when witnessing their severe torture would console them with the words,

"Be patient O family of Yasir, for your final destination is Paradise".

It was said that her son and her husband at times would say a few words to appease the mushrikeen(idol-worshippers) inorder to try to ward off the appalling torture, although they hated to do so. However, Sumayah(ra) never uttered anything the mushrikeen wanted her to say until Abu Jahl in his frustration and rage thrust a spear into her private parts and killed her. With this, she gained the distinction of becoming the first martyr of Islam. She called for the oneness of Allah and the truth of Islam till her dying breath. It is about people like Sumayah(ra) that Allah(swt) says in the Qur'an,

"Verily, Allah has purchased of the believers their lives and their properties for (the price) that theirs shall be the Paradise."   [TMQ 9: 111]

The history of Islam is filled with examples of women who carried the *Da'wah* to Islam and patiently endured whatever trials and suffering this entailed. Many faced severe persecution in the process but such torture never shook their faith nor wavered their determination in carrying the message of Islam to those around them. Umm Shreek al-Qarashiyah al-Aamiriyah was one such woman. She embraced Islam in the early days of the religion and was keen to spread the message of Islam to the Makkan society.

So she would visit the houses of the Quraysh families and invite the women to accept Islam. She would do this secretly to avoid the nobles of the Quraysh from obstructing her call. However, due to the strength of her efforts, her work became known amongst the people of Quraysh who turned her out of Makkah. Those who rode her out of the town placed her on a camel and left her without any food or drink for three days until she began to lose consciousness. Whenever they stopped in their journey, they would leave her out in the burning sun whilst they sought shade and keep food and drink away from her.

Even young girls at the time of the Prophet (saw) displayed their courage and perseverance in supporting the Messenger(saw) in his call and his endeavour to establish the first Islamic state in Madinah. When the Prophet (saw) and his companion Abu Bakr(ra) made the hijra from Makkah to take power in Madinah, they took shelter from the Quraysh during the journey in the cave of Hira at the top of Mount Thawr. It was a young girl - Asma bint Abu Bakr(ra) - the daughter of Abu Bakr who each night would bravely cover the great distance between Makkah and Mount *Thawr*, climbing the mountain to bring food and water to the Prophet (saw) and her father and news of the people who were lying in wait for them.

The difficulty of the journey as well as the presence of watchful enemies did not deter her from performing this daily task for she knew that by protecting the life of the Messenger(saw) and helping him to reach Madinah, she was supporting the *deen* and aiding the establishment of the authority of Islam. In performing this task she was severely tested. One day, the Quraysh surrounded her and asked about her father, placing severe pressure on her but she denied knowing anything. Abu Jahl even struck a heavy blow to her but this did not weaken her resolve in keeping her secret hidden nor in continuing her task of taking provisions and news to the Prophet (saw), appreciating the dangers that this entailed. The Prophet (saw) blessed her with the news of Paradise in the Hereafter for her actions and sacrifices.

These noble women of the past should be taken as role models and sources of motivation for Muslim women today. Their lives are exemplary examples of how they fulfilled all their Islamic responsibilities - as mothers, wives, daughters and *Da'wah* carriers with the utmost effort, zeal, courage and patience and were promised great rewards in the process. It is surely these types of rewards and promises of Jannah that every Muslim women aspires to achieve for the Hereafter. Such hopes and dreams can be fulfilled by following suite in the devotion and characteristics of these noble women in carrying the *Da'wah* to establish the rule of Islam.

Conclusion

Today, in the absence of the Khilafah state, the lives of Muslim women globally have been plunged into darkness. They have been stripped of their dignity and forced to endure unimaginable suffering and pain. As Muslim women Britain, we hear their cries, we feel their pain, their shame is our shame. We understand that it is only by the return of their guardian - the Khilafah that their oppression will be lifted. We therefore have the ability to bring light to those who have lived in darkness for so many years through supporting this call for the return of their shield and protector.

So let us transform our pain, our shame and our tears for our sisters to active work to re-establish the Khilafah state and encourage our families, our childen and our friends to do likewise. Our Ummah bleeds and cries out for us. Let us answer their call. Allah(swt) revealed to Musa(as) that in the Ummah of Mohammed there will be men who stand upon every elevated place and in every valley, calling out the shahadah of La-ilaha-illAllah and that their reward will be that of the Prophets. Let us be of these people.

May the honour of the victory of the return of Allah(swt)'s Law to the world and the magnificent rewards that this work brings in Jannah, be upon the hands of each one of us. Allah(swt) says in Surah Az-Zumar,

"And he who brings the truth and he who confirms (and supports it), such are the men who do right. They shall have all that they wished for in the presence of their Lord. Such is the reward of those who do good."   [TMQ Az-Zumar: 33-34]

www.ingramcontent.com/pod-product-compliance
Lightning Source LLC
Chambersburg PA
CBHW070241290526
45789CB00004B/1716